HOW TO GET HIRED

HOW TO GET HIRED

Insider Secrets to Finding and Getting a Great Job

AUSTIN KELLY AND **GABRIELA KELLY**

Career Crocodile also publishes its books in a variety of electronic formats. Some content that appears in print may not be available in electronic books. For more information about Career Crocodile products, visit our website at www.careercrocodile.com

Printed in the United States of America

"People who rely on a resume without taking the time to meet the boss, never get the job!"

- Austin Kelly

Contents

Introduction

You've probably picked up this book and wondered, what exactly is this How To Get Hired Book? And how will it help me?

The How To Get Hired Book is the Holy Grail for those who desire success in his/her career. Seriously, if there is an end all, be all---then this is it! The How To Get Hired Book establishes the right levels of actions and thinking that guarantee success and ensure that you'll continue operating at these levels throughout your life and career. The How To Get Hired Book will even dissolve fears, increase your courage and belief in yourself, eliminate procrastination and insecurities, and provide you with a sense of purpose that will revitalize your life, dreams, and career goals.

The How To Get Hired Formula is the single principle that all top career achievers are using in the most flourishing areas of their lives. Regardless of how you define a successful career, this book will show you how to guarantee the attainment of it---with any career dream and in any economy. The first thing that has to happen is for you to adjust your mindset and your actions to How To Get Hired every time in any economy. I will show you How To Get Hired thoughts and activities that will make life easier and more fun and will provide you with more time. After spending a lifetime studying career success, I believe the How To Get Hired Formula to be the one ingredient that all successful working professionals know and use to create the careers they desire.

The How To Get Hired Book will show you how to define the correct career goals, accurately estimate the effort needed, discern how to approach your application process with the right frame of mind, and then determine exactly how much action to take. You will see why success in a career is guaranteed when you operate within the parameters of the How To Get Hired Formula, and you will finally understand the single reason why most working professionals never achieve success. You will discover for the first time the mistakes working people make when setting goals that, when done, single-handedly destroys any chance of those career goals becoming a reality. You will also learn how to figure out the precisely right amount of effort necessary to accomplish any career goal---of any size. Finally, I will show you how to make it a habit and discipline to operate at Increased levels. And trust me---once you are doing so, success won't just be guaranteed; it will continue to perpetuate itself, literally producing more career opportunities---and virtually unstoppable job---triumphs.

The How To Get Hired Formula simplifies and demystifies the phenomenon of what a successful career is and what it takes to be successful. Personally, the biggest mistake I've made is failing to set my career goals high enough---in both personal and professional aspects of my life. It takes the same amount of energy to have a great career as it does an average one, just as it takes the same amount of energy and effort to make $100,000 a year as it does $10,000 a year. Sound Crazy? It's not---and you'll see this when you start operating at higher work levels. Your career goals will change, and the actions you take will finally begin to match who you are and what you are capable of doing. You will start taking action(s), followed by more step (s)--- and will achieve what you've set out to do, regardless of the conditions and situations you face in your career. The single most important contributor to the success I have created in my job came as a result of operating with a How To Get Hired Mentality.

The How To Get Hired Formula will ensure your success regardless of your talent, education, financial situation, organizational skills, time management, the industry you are in, or the amount of luck you have. Use this book as though your life and your dreams depended on it, and you will learn to operate at new and higher levels than you ever thought possible!

Chapter 1
How do you Get Hired?

To make it simple, thought it would be a good idea to jump right into things you should get started to Get Hired. The intent of the book is to provide you with what you need to know without any fluff. And to make it an easy to read as possible, so you do not have to hunt down what you need to get you started.

You will also notice, this book has enough space between sentences to write notes; this way you can use this book as a reference to find what you need when you are looking for it.

So let's start with this:

12 Ways to Get Hired Fast

1. Research, the company.
2. Research, the person you are going to meet with for things you have in common. Example: (where they went to school, where they worked before)
3. View the job role and responsibility in detail.
4. Research what you are not an expert in.
5. Research the industry of the company. (Benchmarks, trends)
6. Research the culture. (Social Media) Glassdoor.com

7. Research the salary and reviews of the company in Glassdoor.com

8. The Phone interview - make sure you have your resume memorized and company research complete.

9. The In-Person interview - make sure you have several copies of your resume, have your cell phone turned off, and you are dressed professionally, arrive 15 minutes early.

10. Have prepared questions related to the job in the interviews.

11. Be very polite and professional to the first persons you come in contact. Example: (secretary, HR clerk, receptionist)

12. Have a prepared pitch for the interview "tell me about yourself" open-ended question's to talk about your professional accomplishments.

Reasons why you don't get the job

1. When you hear this sentence you know you are not going to get the job "it has been a pleasure, we are still interviewing other candidates," why because they had other people in mind.

2. The company already had a candidate in mind, and they are going thru the motions to appear fair or to see what is the pool of candidates.

3. The company did not have the job approved in the budget. (must be in the budget that budget is your salary).

4. If you still want the job, volunteer your salary, and undercut your pay against the competition or the person they had in mind. The fact that you agreed to make way less, it is a game changer, they will reconsider you for the job.

Hire Cycle

One good picture of what it takes to look for a job is to think of it as a cycle.

There is a beginning and end; no matter what position you are applying, and how often it is the same cycle. Why!

The job you want takes effort, and you have to know what you want and to know how to get it---it is a series of events.

The Hire Cycle is a series of events, and these events require actions to get the Job you want.

Here is an illustration in the hire cycle

You have proven Tactical roadmap to land your dream job!

1. Research what is needed to get the job.
2. Analyze your findings to see if you are the right fit. If you are not the right fit then actions to do, you need to see what it will take to become the right fit.
3. The Resume has to match the Job you are applying for online.
4. Apply for the job online; apply multiple times for not just one time.
5. The interview requires preparation and practice.
6. Job Offer, what to say what not to say.
7. Start a new job, the new job is a temporary situation, and you always want to promote yourself.
8. Get ready for the next job, start the hiring cycle.

Exercise

What are the two parts of the Hire Cycle?

_____

_____

_____

_____

_____

_____

_____

What are the four reasons why you don't get the job?

_____

_____

_____

_____

_____

_____

_____

Are you ready to Get Hired?

_____

_____

_____

_____

_____

_____

_____

Chapter 2

How do you choose a Career?

D o you have any idea what you want to do for the rest of your life? Here are four insightful questions to ask yourself when you want to change your career.

- Do you want a new Profession?
- Do you want a new Position?
- Do you want a new Title?
- Do you want more Money?

This is an excellent opportunity to step back and reflect. Ask yourself, "If I was going to do something I like and would do it for free, what would that line of work be?"

For example, if you are an office person, sitting in front of a computer all day; and feel you rather be on your feet and like to help people and see that you want to be in the medical profession---this takes a new set of qualifications, job category, and industry when jumping from office to medical.

Another example, if you are a bookkeeper, in this role you create financial transactions (i.e. posting information to accounting journals or accounting software) from documents as invoices to customers, cash receipts, and supplier invoices, plus reconcile accounts to make sure of the accuracy, and want to move up to a CPA, to perform a broader range of accounting, auditing and tax activities as a professional service to both private and public companies—big or small. Then you are not too far off, and it is within the same professional industry and job Category—Accounting. New sets of qualifications are needed to be a CPA.

Do you want to jump from an individual contributor to a supervisor or manager in the same job category? What I mean by job categories is this, the area and profession you are interested in, there are many choices of jobs, see below for some of the different job categories.

Job Category

- Accounting	- General Business	- Other
- Automotive	- Government	- Professional Services
- Banking	- Grocery	- Purchasing - Procurement
- Biotech	- Health Care	- QA - Quality Control
- Broadcast - Journalism	- Hotel - Hospitality	- Real Estate

For example, if you work at a bank as a bank teller, this is best classified as a banking job category.

Now if you are an individual contributor, meaning you have no direct reports, you work alone. And the next job up you want is for a Supervisor or Manager; it's entirely possible you will get the job fairly quickly because it is within the same industry—banking--- and job category of banking.

In this case, there are other factors that only you might be aware of that is going on for an internal move up. The pros are that you have industry and company knowledge of banking. There are minimal cons to moving up within the company, there might be some things you do not know; however, you can find out.

Find out the company policies of being promoted or moving up within the company.

For example, before you apply for the job, let your manager know in your one-on-ones professional performance meetings that you aspire to be in a new role, this way they are not surprised, and they can provide you support and the ground rules of moving up.

Another scenario, if the manager does not support your move because there are no open positions available or you do not meet the requirements of being in your job for 12 or 18 months.

Then start to take an internal assessment of the organizational dynamics, and seek other alternatives. One alternative is to apply internally anyway for similar positions outside the branch, second alternative wait to meet your 12-18 month tenure to transfer to your desired job, third, ask for an exception from your manager to allow you to move, or forth apply outside the company.

a. Going back to the job you want, if it's within the same job category (e.g., banking), or entirely new profession (let's say accounting), it all requires the same step: Research and Analysis.

b. Now if you do not know, what it takes to do that job---Research and Analysis are required. You need to know the facts before investing your money and time in something new.

Exercise

What is the line of work you want to be in?

_____

_____

_____

_____

_____

_____

_____

_____

What are the four questions to ask yourself when you want to change your career?

_____

_____

_____

_____

_____

_____

_____

_____

Fill in the following. If the _____ does not support your move because there are no open positions available. Second alternative wait to meet your _____ month tenure to _____ to your desired position, or forth apply _____ the Company.

Chapter 3

Can You Do the Job?

D o you have sufficient experience, training, education, aptitude, and interest to be productive? Can you deliver what the organization needs from this position? How has your background prepared you for this job? What have you achieved up to now? What do you know about this job and company?

In most job interviews, the majority of interview questions asked by employers are determined whether or not you can do the job for which you are interviewing. If your answers do not demonstrate that you can do the required daily tasks, you will likely not be considered a serious candidate for the job position. Many questions that assess the extent of your qualifications are highly specific nature, differing from job to job and industry to industry, and so are not appropriate for this book. Make sure you are prepared for any job-specific questions that you could be asked. For Example, if you are interviewing for a highly technical job, be ready for technical questions!

For a complete list of questions that address the interviewer's first concern, see chapters 8-9. The primary strategy for dealing with this type of problem is to provide concise and concrete information.

Be sure to do the next Exercises, it will help you take inventory, to see if you can do the job.

Exercise

Do you have sufficient _____, training, _____, aptitude, and _____ to be productive? Can you deliver what the organization needs from this _____?

How has your background prepared you for this new job?

Chapter 4

How do you Search for a Job Online?

The job search efforts have to be established, and you have to plan out your time and energy on how much time you will be dedicated to getting the job you want. Looking for a job can become a full-time job, determine the time of search invested in your online job search.

How often do you Apply Online:

Daily, for example, are you going to dedicate one hour a day, or Weekly, are you going to spend Saturday mornings for your effort or Monthly?

TIP: Take a break after every 20 minutes of job searching online.

To give you an idea of the activities needed to get your job. Dedicate a designated time to job search online, activities include:

- Follow up on emails
- Apply to new job searches
- Research companies for upcoming interviews
- Set aside your suit attire for upcoming interviews
- Print out resumes for upcoming interviews

- Map out your driving directions to upcoming interviews

The job search efforts have to be established and planned out to meet your daily task and goals for you to land your next dream job. Looking for a job can become a full-time job, determine the time of search invested in your online job search.

Exercise

How often do you Apply Online?

_____
_____
_____
_____
_____
_____
_____
_____

Write two examples of activities needed to get you a job?

_____
_____
_____
_____
_____
_____
_____
_____

Chapter 5

How do you Research for a Job Salary?

Research is the process of gathering information and data, When you research for a job salary you want to emerge yourself as the expert on the job category, industry, line of work, education requirements, job qualifications, salary range, the geographic area you want to work and live, and trends.

The research can include talking to your network or other people already doing the line of work you are interested in pursuing. Jump on the Internet, or other means, the quickest method is the Internet. Start your research, look at job sites, including Indeed.com, Glassdoor.com, actual company postings; talk to your friends or professional network to see if they have or know someone in that new job you like to have. In your research find out:

Job Description: sometimes companies have different job titles for the same position. Read those and see how they are the same or different. Identify those differences, save them for when you are doing your analysis.

Job Category: Identify if that job you are interested in is in the same job Category. (I.e., Accounting, healthcare, real estate)

Industry: Identity how many sectors that new job you want is found in. For example, if you're going to be a CPA, you will see that every industry, every company is looking for a CPA across the country. This leads you to a wide range of options. Another example, if you want to be a dental hygienist, the research might lead you only to work in one industry (dental).

Job Demand: How many companies are looking for the same person to fill in the position. Use the keyword of the job title you want can do this. Go to the job boards of Indeed, Monster, and Glassdoor.com—to name a few. Enter the job title in the search criteria, and see how many results you get back. The results will tell you how much the demand is. If the results are low, let's say ten results showed up for the entire county, you know that job description might not be a high need. If the results are high, more than 100 results within the county, you know that everyone is looking for the same skill. In the findings of both high and low demands, identify the salary ranges. We are not concluding yet; even if the market is low, the salary requirements might be high. We are just gathering the information as part of the research. After the study, you will do the analysis, which will help you decide what to do next. Just identify the demand.

Education qualifications: for each job category you find, identify the educational requirements. Does the job require a bachelor's degree, certifications, license, or master's degree? Identify if the degree has to be in a specific major (i.e., communications, accounting, marketing). Sometimes the educational requirements will say "Preferred" (aka Nice to Have, but not required) a degree in XYZ. If this is the case, it is not required, however, a bonus. Do not let the "Preferred" discourage you, continue with the research and identify it as a nice to have for the employer.

Years of experience: Identify the years of experience required for the job you want. Some posts they might be asking for beginners or entry, mid or senior levels. In the beginners or entry level, this will be just out of high school, recent college graduate for two years experience.

The intermediate level usually means between two year to five years of experience in the job doing the same job you are doing now. Senior Level usually means over seven years of experience.

Salary expectations: Identify the salary for each job you are interested in. When searching for a job, many employers list the salary range. If they do not show the pay range, there are several ways to find them.

Try these Tips: 1. Go to indeed, in the search criteria enter a. the job, city, full time, and press find. A new screen pops up; on the left panel there will be salaried estimate ranges and the number of jobs that fall within that salary range. (See the Salary Range Estimate Results list illustration below).

As you can see it list the annual salary and the number of jobs paying that annual salary.

Salary Range Estimate Results List

Salary Estimate

$90,000	(71)
$100,000	(61)
$110,000	(47)
$120,000	(31)
$145,000	(14)

Start looking into each of the salary ranges to see if the results match what you are looking for.

In Indeed, on the left panel, you will also see in the results by Experience, the list shows: Senior, Mid and Entry Level. (Illustration of the Experience Level illustrated below)

Experience Level Results List

Experience Level

Senior Level	(35)
Mid Level	(31)
Entry Level	(11)

If you want to see what the salary ranges are by Experience Level, simply click on the Experience level you believe it right for you.

Start reading each one and identify the salary level for each level.

If you are a college graduate, suggest identifying the salary and job requirements of the entry-level and mid-level experience.

If you go back to indeed, click on an Entry level, new results will show up in the Experience Level.

The results can be narrowed down to show entry level you will find fewer effects. As you can see in the screen shot below:

There are two positions where the salary is over $120,000 a year compared to the previous findings of 14 jobs paying $120,000 a year.

Salary range results **before** pressing "Entry Level" button	Salary range **after** pressing the "Entry Level" button.
Salary Estimate	Salary Estimate
$90,000 (71)	$85,000 (7)
$100,000 (61)	$90,000 (6)
$110,000 (47)	$110,000 (4)
$120,000 (31)	$115,000 (3)
$145,000 (14)	$120,000 (2)

Salary range results before pressing the "Entry Level" button Salary range after pressing the "Entry Level" button.

Salary Range Results Differences Table

- Add this piece of information to your research information gathering. It will give you an idea of what the market is paying.

Analysis: gather all the information from your research together to start the investigation. The best and simple way to put your research together is in a Matrix format. The Matrix format can be done in MS office excel spreadsheet. The reason for this, it is will be easy on the eyes and easy to find and put what you have researched in an organized manner.

TIP: It is best to do an outline in a Matrix format using Microsoft "MS" Office Excel spreadsheet before you start your research.

This way as you do your research, you can fill in the model with your findings. It will make it easier to document what you find. The end goal is to find out the demand for the job, and what it will take for you to reach your goal. Use a Matrix table using MS Excel spreadsheet. Or a piece of paper to draw out the Matrix to help determine your options based your findings from your research:

In the Excel Matrix layout in the header (horizontal):

1. Job Category
2. Job description
3. Industry
4. Job Demand
5. Salary
6. Location
7. Experience
8. Education.

Below is an illustration to give you an idea of how to do the Matrix.

Research and Analysis Matrix Table

Job Category	Job description	Industry	Demand	Salary averge	Location	General Experienc	Education	Certifications	Industry experience
IT	Business Analyst	Banking	high	75,000	Los Angeles	5 years	Bachlors	Some technical	Not always required
Media	Social Media Specialist	Not required	Medieum	35,000	Los Angeles	3 years	Bachlors	Some technical	Not always required
Medical	RN	Medical	high	80,000	Los Angeles	1 year	Registered Nur	some	Yes

Start filling in the Matrix based on your research.

Once you finish fill in your research findings into the excel spreadsheet, stop and analyze the research. The research you have done has now been done into pieces of data. While looking at the data, see if there are any patterns.

Ask yourself: what is typical for this position I want.

- Is it the education, or experience?
- Is the demand higher in one city instead of this other city or state?
- Does this job exist only in one industry?
- Are there any differences in the education and salary levels?

Identify what is common?

After you do your research by filling in your Matrix table make a comparison between your Analysis and you.

The "YOU" is essential. You need to know your current standings of education, experience, and what you WANT. By identifying where you are, it will make it easier to see the GAPs you have to fill in to reach your goal.

Create a new MS Office Matrix, use the same header (horizontal) information from the research: That is, in the excel layout in the header:

- Job Category
- Job description
- Industry
- Job Demand
- Salary
- Location
- Experience
- Education

In one of the cells (vertical) type in ME, below the battery, type in New Job, In the ME column, start filling in your current situation for each of these:

Job Category: what is the current job category you are in.

Job description: what is the job description you currently have?

Industry: what is the industry you are currently in?

Job Demand: is the job demand high or low?

Salary: what is the salary range you make from the job?

Location: what city or county is your job located.

Experience: how many years have you been in your current job description?

Education: what degrees, licenses, and certification you have to earn?

Let's focus on the job you want. Below "ME" in the excel spreadsheet type in "New Job" in the cell for the new Job you want. In the New Job column, start filling in with what you identified as being typical for the job you want:

Job Category: what is the job category your desired position falls in?

Job description: what is the typical job description used for the job you want?

Industry: what is the industry the new job you want falls in?

Job Demand: is the job demand high or low?

Salary: what is the salary ranges?

Location: where are most of the jobs you want to be located?

Experience: what is the standard year of experienced my new job is requiring?

Education: what degrees, licenses, and certifications do my new job need?

Identify the gaps (i.e., weak links and holes) and determine do you have enough to get you the job. If not what do you need to do to close the gaps? Determine what you have and target your post. If you do not have lots of differences, move on to match your resume to the job description, and if applicable of the industry. The next chapter will tell you how to match your resume to the job you are capable of doing.

For your convenience, the table below is an example of a comparison between the new Job you want and YOU:

For instance, to best illustrate the comparison, I am profiling you as a Content Specialist in the job category of Media. If you want to be in Media, this is how the table would look for you.

Look at the "Me" and "New Job" row, highlighted in yellow; the yellow represents the commonality and matches between your current job and the job you want. The goal of the Matrix is to identify the "gap" meaning what are you missing to get the new Job.

In this illustration the gaps between you and your new job are:

- Salary: your original post makes more
- Demand: there is a higher demand for your new job you want
- Education: A bachelor's degree is required.

Gap Matrix Table

	Job Category	Job description	Industry	Demand	Salary average	Location	General Experience	Education	Certifications	Industry experience
Me	Media	content specialist	Not required	low	30,000	Los Angeles county	2 years	None	Google Analytics, and other media	eCommerce
New Job	Media	Social Media Specialist	Not required	Medium	35,000	Los Angeles county	3 years	Bachelors	Google Analytics, and other media	Not always required

If you do have lots of gaps, take a step back. See how close can you get to the job you are looking for. Here are a couple of suggestions:

Based on the results:

Can you get a lower level position within the same job category or industry, and do you continue to stay at your current job (that is, job category or industry) until you can close the gaps to move you up to the next step up.

Whatever your decision is, take your options and make a Pro/Con list personalized to you. We will use the Media example to illustrate how to come up with a decision. Below is a Decision table to help evaluate the pro/cons of your next step if you have gaps in getting the job you want.

TIP: use MS Office Excel spreadsheet to do the Pro/Cons Matrix table

Take a new position at an Entry level for the Job I want (Social Media Specialist)		Stay at current job	
Pro	Con	Pro	Con
Get the experience and on the job training to gain that experience	The pay scale is lower from what I make now or the same.	Keep my salary range	I will not be able to move up
Get paid for learning at an entry level position			Do not gain the job experience of the new job I want as Social Media Specialist
		Allow time to earn a bachelor degree without jeopardizing my salary and current job stability	

Pros and Cons Matrix table

	Gaps	What is needed to close the gap
Job Category:	No	Within the same job category
Job description	Yes	Job descriptions are slightly different.
Industry	No	Does not matter job needed across industries
Demand	No	This is a Pro, the demand is high for this job
Salary	Yes	New job pays more
Location	No	jobs are within the same city
Experience	Yes	Need more experience
Education	Yes	Bachelor's degree

Both options are right, it depends on the new job you want and if financially you can afford either opportunity. The next steps are on you. What do you want to do next? Do you want to close the gaps found in the analysis between you and your new job?

What is keeping you away from your new job?

Using the prior example, if the new job you want is Social Media Specialized, what do you need to do to close the gap to get that job you want.

Use this list to identify the gaps and what is needed to close them:

Closing the Gap List table

For Social Media Specialized, there are four gaps. Job Description, Salary, Experience, and Education. In your analysis, you identified what was required to get the job. And find that a degree is necessary, that is the gap that needs to be closed. The remaining three holes can be closed with time doing volunteering or part-time jobs to gain that experience.

You can't go wrong with earning your bachelors degree; this will open the door to more opportunities. In your analysis, you will find that the majority of employers require a bachelor's degree. At the end of this, you should know how close or far away you are from the job you want. The research and analysis conducted help narrow down the gaps in the position you want. The Matrix's done for them, and even the pros/cons Matrix will direct you to the next steps of your action plan.

In summary, chapter two is asking you to find out "what job you want."

The answer is not simply because you do not know what if it is realistic. This chapter asks you to find out what you want by doing some research, research the job categories, industry, the demand for that job you want, what are the educational requirements. Once you have that all written down, start the analysis.

To help in the analysis, a Matrix table in MS office can serve as your template. It will be used to organize the data from your research.

Once the data is organized you can do a Gap Analysis (i.e., what are you missing to get that job). Us the other Matrix table covered as a template too, it will provide to lay out the Pros/Cons of your present situation and give you an idea of what it will take to pursue that job you want.

In the end, step back reflect on your findings and say "what is keeping me from that job I want."

Exercise

Write down an example of pros and cons when you take a new position at an Entry level Job.

Write down an example of pros and cons when you stay at current job.

What are you missing to get the job you want?

Chapter 6

How do you write an Excellent Resume?

T he topic covered in this chapter is how to write an excellent resume and match the job you want with your resume. The assumption is you have gone through the exercise covered in previous Chapters, and you can do the job.

How to match your job to your resume.

- You identified the job you want; you did the research and analysis and recognized and closed the gaps taking you away from the position you want.
- If you have not closed the gaps, at least you know what they are and soon will be closed to get you the job you want.

Step 1)

First, look at the job descriptions of the job you want.

- Use recruiting platforms like Indeed, Monster or company job boards. Update your research and analysis if you see the job requirements have changed. Identify the commonality between the job descriptions and job titles.

In each of the job descriptions, qualifications and requirements identify common keywords that you need to highlight.

Step 2)

Look at other resumes for the job you want.

Visit some of the search engine job boards or on the Internet. Indeed, you can search for resumes. Use those as a reference point to see what others are holding your job say on their resume. Please note, this is only for reference, do not copy someone else's resume. The goal is to give you an idea of what they are putting on their resume to make it easy for you to put your together.

Your Resume:

Resume Design: there are many Design's available. Use the one you think will fit your experience and education. Considering you reviewed other resume designs online, use the format that is most relevant in the job category or industry you want to work in.

Your resume should always have these sections:

- Contact Information
- Summary
- Skills
- Work Experience (chronological order)
- Education (chronological order)

Additional relevant information if you need to fill your resume out more. This may include, volunteering, committee member, or awards/nominations.

TIP: Here is one thing no one will tell you about your resume, the first two pages of your resume should have 75% of the keywords on the job description. This is the norm across the industry.

Insider secret: all jobs are posted on the Internet. All the posted jobs are supported in a Human Resource Recruiting System. When the employer posts the position, that employer will scan your resume when you submit your job application.

The employer has a setup date range of when to stop taking job submission/applications. The web forms have your resume (it can be attached, or you built it out in their system). When the end date arrives, the system automatically scans all the job submissions with their resume.

The automatic scan has logic built in based on criteria set by the employer's recruiter. The standard criteria are to short-list the top resumes that match 75% of the keywords.

For example, if there were 500 resumes submitted, and of those 500, only 20 job applications met 75% of the keywords. Those 20 job applications will move forward to the Recruiter to review. Have as many keywords as possible, at the same time make it look organized by having headers at the top of your resume.

Tip: The headers should include the keywords the job you want is repeatedly highlighting in the job description.

For example, if the job you want is a Social Media Specialist, use Media as a header, and write every skill, trend, tool, everything you worked on that is media specific keywords match the job you want. Even if the employers use different software, use the same words. Remember, there are many tools, software or even equipment that do the same thing.

Another example: if you have used Salesforce.com Customer Relationship Management (CRM) in the past and had it in your resume; and the job you are applying for uses SAP Customer Relationship Management (CRM); make sure this wording "Customer

Relationship Management (CRM)" is in your resume. It is a keyword; and the system will recognize it.

TIP: use this wording repeatedly, this way the system will recognize it; giving you a high match percentage (%)

Resume Header: an image of an example of a header in your resume:

The red box is the header.

Tip: Make these critical words in **bold** and must be on the first page. Again use keywords, these will be recognized in the system, and catch the eye of the recruiter

Tip: In the header, add the job titles for the job you want. Companies use different job titles, but it is for a similar position or role within the same job category or classification.

Tip: Here is an example of the Jobs Titles in large font, the next line is the keywords used in all the jobs in the industry, job title and job description for the jobs.

Resume Header First Page outline:

Header first page

Global Marketing/Product/Project Management Executive

Digital Marketing – Communications - Media – Project / Product Management, Salesforce - IT platforms

Different headers for different jobs: Depending on the position you want, the header will have to be changed to match up keywords. These keywords are usually the latest trend, try to keep up with your industry and profession to use the new "term" be prepared to have several version of your resume. I have five different resumes with different wording on the header.

Multiple resumes: be prepared to have a different version of your resume because each company created their own and unique job description with requirements. The reason for this, the recruiter ask the hiring managers to develop and write up the job title, job description, responsibilities, and the type of education needed to meet the role the hiring manager is looking for.

Tip: In essence, many times the job description, education and experience required are all the same across companies, what makes each job different is these companies do not use the same words when they advertise for the position.

It is essential to know each of these companies uses different keywords known within their unique industry, company, department, location, and workgroup. As you are looking for your job, and start to read the job responsibilities and descriptions, after a while you will be able to see a pattern. You will be able to see what is familiar and what is internal company terminology.

For example, one resume might be geared toward the entertainment industry. Use keywords, and highlight skills more likely to be required in this industry (i.e., marketing, sales, analytics). Have another resume for the retailer industry, and your resume should reflect critical words used in the retailer industry (i.e., e-commerce and sales)

Resume Name convention: when you have multiple resumes to match the job you want. It is best to have several version of your resume. This means each of your resumes should have a unique naming convention. The naming convention is essential so that when you get called for the job, you have a good idea which position you are getting a callback.

For example: let say you have five resumes for different companies.

The reason for the different resumes is because each company had the same job title, but different keywords in their job description.

To make sure you were a good match for each of the jobs you applied for you have to create five resumes with different naming conventions. This way when you get a call back from the company you know which resume you used to in the application submission process.

Five examples on how to save your resume

1) Marketing Coca-Cola
2) Marketing Johnson and Johnson
3) Marketing Amazon.com
4) Marketing Warner Brothers
5) Marketing City of Pasadena

Insider Secret: Different industries and jobs have their keywords, it is essential to customize your resumes to that industry or job category if one resume cannot meet the typical 75% percentile of the criteria the company is looking for, that person's resume will get a rejection letter

In critical words there is a difference between an Administrative Assistant and Coordinator.

Administrative Assistant keywords in general are: Generate memos, emails, and reports.

Coordinator keywords are Ensure that project documents are complete, current, and stored. In short, Coordinator and Administrative Assistant vary by industry, and it could be a marketing coordinator or marketing assistant, IT (information technology) coordinator, or IT Administrative Assistant. You have to read and customize your resume using those words.

We all know you can do the job; you have to trick the HR Recruiting system that **YOU** are **PERFECT**.

Of course, the font and format have to be balanced, meaning, your name, the phone number must be centered. If you have any designations (i.e., an abbreviation of the degree or certification or license), add them right after your name.

Mine is: Austin Kelly, BA, CSM, CGA, see illustration below.

This is what the abbreviations stand for in my Resume Header on the first page.

- BA stands for my Bachelors in Science.
- CSM stands for Certified Scrum Master
- CGA stands for Certified Google Analytics

If you have a Master Degree, add MS, or MBA. If you have a certification, add the designation it.

The company sets the percentage match, the standard is 75% as a threshold, this has been my experience is what companies use at a minimum.

Insider Secret: As soon as you see the job, apply now.

Companies also have a job submission cut off. Some companies have a cut off of 500 or 1,000 submissions per job. These cut off are not all the same; they are settings in the HR system. The company or recruiter provides the criteria to their Information Technology (i.e., IT) to set.

For example, during the housing bubble recession, companies where getting slammed with resumes, over 1,000 resumes for each open job requisition. Many companies started to put a cutoff limit because there were too many submissions. The most common cut off limit was 1,000 resumes per job. Remember, the HR system identifies the first set of job candidates based on percentage match. Out of the 1,000 job submissions 10-25% of the job applicants where percentage matches.

Resume Header: Gone are the days a recruiter or hiring manager read a resume. Now we have computers. For the past 15 years companies (big or small) have been using Human Resource Recruiting Systems to match resumes to their open job requisition. Rarely is a recruiter or hiring manager reviews your resume first.

This next part is to give you an idea of the Application process. Processes vary, this is the typical process your resume goes through to get you the Hiring Life Cycle.

Here is the typical process:

Process 1: Once you submit your resume, the Human Resource Recruiting system does a match of keywords from using the first page and second page of your resume.

Inside secret: the recruiter or hiring manager establishes HR system criteria and settings, they determine the standards and requirements in the HR system, which their IT department will set in the order. One of the IT System settings will include: how many pages of your resume will scan (typically first three). The other criteria and requirements may consist of: Cut off limit, this is when the maximum number of job submissions are reached (e.g., the cut off is 1,000 job submissions for this job) no longer accepting job submissions.

Cut of date, this is the date when job submissions are no longer being accepted. The percentage of word matches to the open job requisition (e.g., save in a particular folder all job submissions or resumes that match 75% of the open job)

Process 2: After the cutoff date or cut off limit met. The Recruiter or hiring manager is notified electronically that their queue or folder is ready for review. Their particular folder will have all the candidates job submission, which have been filtered, or shortlisted-based on the HR system criteria set in the HR system.

Process 3: The recruiters will only look at the filtered or shortlisted resumes where the minimum percentage (let us say their threshold is 75%) match to the job requisitions. I mean 75%, again the % is determined by the requirements of the hiring manager, recruiter or company. The percentage can range from 70 to 95% resume to job description match.

Process 4: The recruiter's reviews by scanning the resumes. I say scan because, in my experience, the Recruiters do not read the resume, they are looking at critical words for the job they are trying to fill.

Insider secret: Recruiters do not want to look bad; they want to be known for finding the perfect candidates. Recruiting is tough, and they have a high turnover. The safest bet for the recruiters (new or seasoned) is going to rely on the HR system to find their candidates. Recruiters do not know enough about the job itself to make a sound judgment if the resume is a good candidate; again they use keywords and the percentage match the HR system provided.

Recruiter ends up down selecting the top 10 resumes they think is the best match. After this, they start to read your resume. During this process, they have the authority not to select your resume, even if it was a 100% job match. Recruiters are humans, and can be biased, or have a perception of you without even knowing you, or are multi-tasking and can overlook and miss qualified candidates

For example, let's say you are 100% match and have a stellar pedigree (e.g., you went to Yale); you have worked for Fortune 10 companies, and went to an Ivy League school. Their bias could be—without talking to you---they may think that you want too much money, or they are not a fit because everyone in the company went to a competing school or the company only has employees from community colleges, or the recruiter might have a self-belief that you might be too sharp and assume you will leave the company as soon as you find something better, etc.…

Process 5: The Recruiter has selected their short list of their top 10 candidates; they are ready for the next step.

Process 6: The recruiter starts contacting the candidates for phone interviews. There are a couple of people that will contact you: A. the recruiter, B. Recruiting coordinator, C. a company in dire need will have the Hiring Manager call you directly.

Process 7: The Recruiter or someone on behalf of the Recruiter will contact you to set up a Date and Time to have a Phone Interview.

In summary, this chapter is about putting your resume together to make it the best match for the job you want. It is a different type of research and analysis at the job description level. This is where you look at common patterns in critical words used for the job you want. Also, reference other resumes to give you an idea of what your competition has on their resume—we do not copy—it is a reference. The important take away is finding all the keywords used for the job description, responsibilities and industry. The result will lead you to have many differences between enterprise and company. This is where it is essential to have more than one resume. You must have multiple resumes targeting the jobs you want. Also added the Application process to give you insight what your resume must go through to get you hired.

Exercise

Write down the name of job boards recruiters use to seek job candidates.

_____
_____
_____
_____
_____
_____
_____
_____

Write down the job submission cut off limit per job posting.

_____
_____
_____
_____
_____
_____
_____
_____

Fill in the following. The first two pages of your resume should have _____ of the keywords on the job description.

Chapter 7

How do you get a Job Interview?

Where to apply? There are many ways to looking and apply for jobs online. The usual go-to place is job websites. Indeed.com, Monster.com, and Glassdoor.com You can also be creative, there are other creative ways to look and apply for jobs: Go on Google and type in the job title you want, go thru the results which are typical: Indeed.com, Glassdoor.com, and Linkedin.com. Scroll down and see if any interest you

TIP: as you find the jobs, look at the job posting to get familiar with what the company who published the situation is looking for, look for commonality. This exercise will make it easier to recognize down the road as you are refining your resume to fit the job.

During the process of putting your resume together helped you recognize your strengths and accomplishments. Now let's look at how the job matches you. To the best of your knowledge, answer the following questions with a specific role in mind. Don't expect to know all the answers now – many you will know in time.

Knowing your target market: As you are searching for your job, ask yourself these questions to see the type of companies you want to work for that will be the perfect fit for you.

- How is the company a fit for you and your skills
- How is the department a fit for you and your skills?
- What are the job requirements?
- How are the company goals, specific projects, and industry challenges, going to align and match you and your skills?
- How is the company, or department values, culture, expectations a fit for you and where you want to be in your career
- How close is the application Match between you and the market?
- Match your skills with the position.
- Determine if there is a match with values and culture.

For example, if you do not support abortion, then you would not apply at a clinic that performs abortions.

Match your skills with desired knowledge, skills, and experience. In your resume, you should have a section listing your knowledge, skills, and experience.

TIP: In the skill section of your resume: list all the skills you have, be sure it is the same wordings the company you are applying for is using.

For this skill section Research and Analysis exercise, you can use the Matrix covered in prior Chapters to help identify what your resume is against the job you are applying for. This will make it easier to recognize the difference. The difference can be the word.

For example: In the education section, the job posting might have the word Bachelors spelled out; and in your resume you have it abbreviated.

Below is an example of the Matrix outline to help you identify the match between you and the job, refer to **New Job Matrix, & Me** illustration.

New Job Matrix, & Me

	Job description	Industry	Salary	Experience required	Education	Preferred Experience	Skills
Me							
Job							

Now with your Matrix, you can see the differences between the job you are applying for and yourself. By category here are some of the characteristic differences.

TIP: this can make a big difference when your resume is scanned in the HR System. It might be flagged as a relevant keyword. And if it is missed because of the abbreviation, you will not be selected as a possible candidate.

Job Description:

My current job description and duties match the job I am Appling for, but not my job title.

TIP: Apply for the job; change your job title on your resume to match the job title the company is looking for. When you get the job offer, and you are asked to complete the job application. In the job application put your actual Job title from the company you work or worked for.

Insider secret: The recruiter and hiring manager do not do the job verification of employment. Once you get the job offer, you are asked to fill out the job application. The job application is then given to:

A) Outsourced to an Employment Screening company, such as Hire Right, and Good Hire.

B). Some HR clerk or coordinator is given the task to screen and verify your employment or degrees.

C). Some smaller companies give the file to the Administrative Assistant to call and do the employment screening.

Insider secret: the recruiter and hiring manager do not talk to the Employment Screeners. Your employment screening is handed off to the next person in the process.

My current experience in the industry (e.g., marketing) matches my industry knowledge the job I am applying for, but the education and certifications do not match me.

Insider secret: if a certificate is keeping or preventing you from qualifying for the job, you can:

A) write in you have the certification and state you will get it by a particular month; or,

B) use this to write in your resume "candidate" for XYZ certification.

The reason you want to do this, you want the HR System to identify you as a match. If you have the exact certification, you increase your chances of making it to the next level...that is the Recruiter.

TIP: In your resume, add that certification in several places. Add it after your name as a designation. In the Education or Certification section, and a Job summary, Job experience (how it was utilized in your job)

Here are some examples of what you can put in your resume:

1) After your name: Austin Kelly, Certified XYZ

2) In the Header: Certified in XYZ

3) Education/Certifications: two options if you have not earned the Candidate yet.

   • Option one looks like this: Education/Certification: Certification XYZ, expected Month/Year.

   • Option Two looks like this: Candidate, Certification XYZ

4) Job summary: used by Certification of XYZ in the capacity of X (e.g., supervisor, Advisor, Subject Matter specialist)

5) Job Description: Applied my knowledge as a Certified XYZ to perform these specialized duties

Only recommend this if you were intending to pursue the certification. Sometimes one cannot register for the certification for lack of money or timing. If you have the means, register for the certification. It does not matter where you get your certification, and it can be online or in a community college, or university. As long as you get it, it will open the door to getting the job you want.

If you get the job offer, quickly register for the certification. During the Employment screening, if the employer asked for proof that you are certified, state that you are a candidate, and if you registered, give them a copy of the registration as proof.

If you do not have the proof, state: I have identified the course where I will be taking the certification, was waiting to get paid before signing up.

After a while, you will not need the Matrix. The Matrix's are baby steps to get you to know what jobs are going to be the right fit. After spending a couple of hours of looking for the right job, going thru the Me & New Job Matrix, updating your resume to match the position, it all becomes second nature.

Applying for a job is not a one-time event, it takes lots of time and commitment. It is not easy looking for a job; it is practically a full-time job to look for a job. What matters is the quality of your resume, what this means, making sure you look like the Perfect Match by having the right percentage of keywords.

TIP: the quality of your resume is substantially matching the keywords of the job you are applying for to your resume. If you use the same resume over and over without double-checking the phrase match, the chances of getting called are low.

The number of job submissions matters, the volume is significant. Think about marketing and advertising, and companies do not advertise one time; companies use various marketing channels to promote their products so consumers can buy their products. In this case, you are the product, the more you apply for jobs, the higher the chance you will get contacted by the company.

TIP: Have several versions ready of your resume. The release of your resume should be by job title or industry. Before submitting your job application, always look to see which one of your multiple resumes you should provide. If you have to change the keywords in your resume to match the job, be sure to make a new version of your resume. Use the job title and company as in the naming convention when you "Save As" the resume.

In summary, the resume tricks are things no one tells you. Your resume has to be pretty, consider it as art. When you have a skill, it will catch the eye of the reader, and make them remember you. Another trick applies right away to the job opening. As soon as you see it APPLY, there is a cut off when an application is no longer being accepted. Behind the scenes, the hiring process, these are processes the recruiter goes through, what they read and what they think makes you a good match for the job. Try and put yourself in their position, to give you a better perspective when working on your resume. When applying for the right job, knowing the right fit takes effort, in using the "Me & Job Matrix" should help you close the gaps to increase your chances of getting the job. There are creative ways to make you be the Perfect Fit if you apply the Tips about quality, and the volume of the posts you are applying for.

Exercise

What are some required keywords for you to be selected as a possible candidate.

_____
_____
_____
_____
_____
_____
_____

Why is it better to consider your resume as a work of art?

_____
_____
_____
_____
_____
_____
_____

What are some creative ways to make you be the Perfect Fit for the job you want?

_____
_____
_____
_____
_____
_____

Chapter 8
You Got a Phone Interview!

C ongratulations your resume has made it to the next phase in the job submission process. The HR System identified you as having met the search criteria percentage established by the company. Now your resume has been filtered and put on the Recruiters or Hiring Managers to work list of possible qualified candidates.

The next step is for the Recruiter or Hiring Manager to review the filtered list in their work queue or list. After they give it the first pass, they will start identifying which job candidates is the best fit for the criteria they are looking to hire for. The Recruiter will identify approximately— the top 5 to 10 candidates. The Recruiter will dedicate the first half of their days calling candidates.

If they cannot reach the job candidate by phone, the next step is the Recruiter will do is send the job candidate an email to see what is the job candidate's availability to talk for about 30 minutes for a phone screen.

The first phone call: when you are actively looking for a job, try not to pick up the phone as soon as it rings, especially if you have been applying to a lot of posts. It will be difficult to remember what you applied for, and what you put on your resume.

TIP: Avoid being off guard, and not knowing what job you applied for. The best is to let the Recruiter or Hiring Manager leave a message. In the letter they will tell you:

1. Who they are.

2. What position they are calling you for.

This way when you call them back, you will be prepared and ready to address their responses.

TIP: Avoid picking up the phone from a recruiter while you are at your current workplace.

You do not want to give a hint to your current employer you are looking to leave for a better opportunity. In case there are layoffs or downsizing, you will be the first one to go if they know you are seeking. Also, some companies have policies if they know you are looking, they will release you that day.

TIP: Keep your job search secret from co-workers. Even if you confide in them. It it is human behavior that they will want to tell someone; even if they do not tell anyone, you will always be thinking, "Did they tell anyone that I am looking?" To be on the safe side and remove any doubts, keep the job search to yourself.

The first email: If the Recruiter could not get a hold of you, they will send you an email asking you several questions:

1). What is your availability they would like to schedule an interview

2). Are you still available and searching for a job

Do not be surprised if some Recruiters even have a list of questions before they also talk to you over the phone. For example, I had several Recruiters give me up to 10-15 items. And if they felt I met that I answered the questions, then they would talk to me. In another example, I had to take a test, and if I passed, they would schedule a phone interview.

In either event, if you are looking for a job, and that is the job you are Perfect for, you will respond to the Recruiter's request. I know I did.

Exercise

What should you avoid from a recruiter while you are at your current job.

_____

_____

_____

_____

_____

_____

_____

_____

How are recruiters filtering out job candidates?

_____

_____

_____

_____

_____

_____

_____

_____

Fill in the following. When you are actively looking for a job, try _____ the phone, especially if you have been applying at a lot of jobs.

Chapter 9

How do you Answer Phone Interview Questions?

Interview Greetings

When you finally connect with the Recruiter and get a chance to talk, start the conversation casually. Ask them open-ended questions, such as "how are you, how is your day, how is the weather in your part of the country" this makes them more at ease and helps lead into a good rapport.

In the call, the Recruiter ask you questions, the questions, below are possible questions they will ask, and your best response:

Question and Answers Table

Question	Answer	Insider Secret
What is your salary requirement	"What is your salary Range?" Once they reply say this: a) yes, that is within my range. b) No, based on the duties, the range is too low, can we go up to $$$$. Can we meet in the middle? Might be able to work with it if I could work remote 2 days out of the week.	Do not say the first number; have them give the salary range. You do not want to go to high or low. Only you know what you need, if you do not have anything, you might say yes, totally up to you. Or even ask to go a little higher. If you have a job, and the move is a promotion, weigh your options of the pros and cons. To see if it worth getting a new job. If the salary is to low, see if they can flexible, by giving you extra paid vacations, working remote, etc.
Why are you leaving your current company	My company outsourced, moved out of state, or is firing off people.	Recruiters think something is wrong with you (a job seeker) for wanting to leave their current job. And when you do not have a job (i.e. layoff) they still think something is wrong with you.
Tell me what you are currently doing	Give them your 1 minute elevator speech	When you start the job hunting, have your elevator speech ready and practice it out loud.
What is your availability to interview	Provide a brief response, "let me check my calendar." Give them your availability	Many times they have the schedule, all you need to do is tell them if you are free that date/time. If you have to check, tell them to give you what they have available,

		try to check while you are on the phone. If you cannot because you do not have your work calendar in front of you, tell them you will get back to them with your availability ASAP.

After the call with the Recruiter, if they ask you "do you have any questions," you say yes, "What are the next steps." You want to know this information to see where you stand in the recruitment process.

Short List of Candidates: When the Recruiter is done with the first set of phone screening, they will make up their short list to three to five candidates they felt where the best fit for the job they are hiring for.

Again the recruiters are human and want to look good to the manager on the candidates picked. They would base their short list of three or so candidates if they met the requirements in the criteria percentage match, your personality, communication skills, and how articulate you were on the phone. The shortlist will be presented to the Hiring Manager. How the short list is given to the Hiring Manager depends on the companies Recruiting policies and procedures.

Here are some possible scenarios of how the shortlists of job candidates are reviewed. What happens next is the Recruiter schedules a meeting with the Hiring Manager.

1. The Recruiter will meet and talk to the Hiring Manager to give them an overview of each candidate they speak to.
2. The Recruiter will email or push the short list of candidates from the HR System into the Hiring Managers queue or work list for them to review.

The Hiring Manager can then share the short list with his team members to help identity which candidates they want to interview.

Once the Hiring Manager goes through the short list, they will contact the Recruiter and provide them with their feedback. The feedbacks can filter the top leading job candidates they want to interview. Or they will tell the Recruiter to look for more candidates. The reasons may vary as to why the Recruiter has to go back to the drawing board.

From my experience:

- After the hiring managers read the candidates resume, they felt where to overqualified, or under qualified.
- They have all ten skills but missing 1 out of the 10.
- There is no need for the position, and the Hiring manager is willing to keep it open, and if they can't find what they are looking for, they will close the job requisition.

When there is a need, there is a callback. When the Hiring Managers does give the green light to the Recruiter to move forward with the top candidates, the Recruiter goes to work and started contacting the leading candidates for the next step in the recruiting process the interview with hiring manager.

In summary, you met the HR System criteria and getting to the first phone screen with the Recruiter or Hiring Manager, which is tough to reach, Congratulations on the Milestone. The first phone call from the recruiter is essential, how and when you answer the call matters. You always want to anticipate a call, be careful when picking up the phone, if you can take the call do ONLY if you are in the right place and have high confidence you know what position. If you have been applying various companies with different jobs; or you are at work, or if you are in a noisy place---do not pick up the phone. When you do pick up the phone or call back the Recruiter, you will be ready, by that time, you will be in a quiet and private location and know exactly what company and job the Recruiter is calling you on. After the call, always ask the recruiter for the next steps, this way you know where you stand in the recruiting process.

Exercise

What is your salary requirement?

Why are you leaving your current company?

What should you ask the recruiter after the end of a phone interview?

Chapter 10

You Got an In-Person Interview!

It is time to get ready for your In-Person interview, here is a list to do's:

1. Print your resume; if you are meeting with a panel of 5 take six resumes with you.
2. Take a binder with a note pad and pen.
3. What to wear for the interview.
4. Wear traditional formal clothes—like if you where running for political office.

Men: IBM look, aim for a blue suit and white shirt, with a nice red, yellow or green tie.

Women: Again IBM looks blue suit and white shirt or blouse. One-inch heels. Minimal make up…do not want to listen too pretty. If you are interviewing with women, you do not want to look too pretty. Women by nature are insecure; and you do not want to be a threat to then, both in brains and looks.

Women: Get a manicure; conservative, plain or natural color...no bright colors (i.e., pink, red, black) your hair should be conservative and to the side. Try and look like a professor.

Men and Women: Your breath, take some mints before the interview; you do not want to have bad breath.

- Wear glasses, and it makes you look smarter.
- Cell Phone: before the interview turn off your cell phone
- Water: if possible, take a small bottle of water, some companies might not offer you any. You will get dehydrated and very unaffordable if you get thirsty.

Questions after the interview: have at least three items ready for you to ask. Even if you know the answer, do not leave the meeting without asking at least two questions. It will show that you are interested in the position.

Most of the jobs people are hiring a worker bee; they are not looking for a leader...even if they say it, do not mean it. In the end, they want to be the leader and do not want any competition.

Have you ever wondered, how did this person get that job...well the hiring manager did not want anyone better than them? They hired B player (person) instead of an A player (person).

Definition:

A Player is: superstar

B Player is a worker bee.

TIP: Practice your lines for your In-Person interview. There are two forms of interviews practiced in the industry: Non-Situational and Situational Behavior.

Non-Situational - Typical questions

There are typical interview questions companies ask, some just question, and some are Behavioral and situational based. It is essential you practice so when you are being interviewed, they flow better, and you think less on how to answer.

These are several typical In-Person interview questions:

If you can memorize at least three of your interview questions, you can master the art of interviewing with practice.

Typical Interview Questions	Interview Responses
Tell me about yourself	I've been in this field for 15 years, I am a team player with strong interpersonal skills and the ability to effectively interact at all levels of management.
What is your weakness	I am a perfectionist, like everything to be perfect, I recognize it is important to step back and assess what is needed to move forward and there are opportunities to improve on the original thought or product or solution.
Why should I hire you	I am committed to the success of the organization, I am confident with my background in (insert your expertise) I can grow and provide shared value.
Have you had a bad boss	I have never had a bad boss, however, I have worked with difficult people. The important thing to remember is what I can do for the growth of the company.

Behavioral and Situational

Behavioral and situational questions follow this simplified version of the framework on how to address Behavioral and Situational type of questions. Leverage this framework by customizing and inserting what is relevant to your experience.

Behavioral and Situation Framework

1. The objective of the task or project.
2. List the specific steps taken to resolve the problem.
3. What was accomplished.
4. What was learned from the experience?

TIP: prepare by have at least three frameworks already written out and start practicing. The reason to have three is if you are interviewing with three different people, you cannot use the same situation to tell your story.

Question	Response
Tell me a time when a project failed	1. The task type was operational 2. An urgent policy had to be implemented in less than 3 days. 3. The steps to implement where a. gather the legal specifications, b. craft the communication with legal, HR and management review; and confirm the distribution list with HR 4. The communication was sent within the timeline and approvals. What failed, the newly acquired company employees where not on the distribution list?

	5. What we learned was to have a consolidated database for HR to have the actual list of employees.
Tell me a time when a project was successful	1. Developed a new product demanded by the market
	2. The steps were to look at new technology and material, study and prove it works, developed a business case to receive funding, did a pilot and trial.
	3. The trial results were positive and profitable; we deployed the product to the market.
	4. What we learned is to constantly assess each phase to mitigate loss and risk.

Insider secret: After the interview, the three people who interviewed you will share to see if you used the same situational story. One of the rules of this type of interview is, **you cannot use the same situational story twice.**

If you repeat the same project or challenge or task to each of the interviewers, you will **automatically be disqualified**. Even if you are perfect, those are the rules and to be fair with all candidates, they are followed.

Why companies use Behavior and Situational questions for interviews tell their situational scenario. According to several articles and recruiters that I have worked with, it serves as an indicator of what the candidate says in the interview, not the resume, by seeing how the candidate's prior experience relates to the job.

Focus on actions and predictions of future behavior. The questions placed are a hypothetical situation to see the response. Evaluates the candidate's ability to apply knowledge and skills to conditions on the next job. In short, gives a good representation of your behavior to determine a pattern on how well you handle a situation in the future at the company.

Practice and practice for the interview, practice for both the Non-situational and the Situational and Behavior.

Your homework is to:

Write your interview questions and responses

- One sheet of paper for Non-situation; and, the other for the Situational and Behavioral questions
- Print out or have it handy in a smart device.
- Sit down in a quiet place and start practicing,

To Do's:

1. Read it silently first
2. Read your questions and responses out loud
3. Memorize your responses
   a. Practice in front of a mirror by responding to the questions
   b. Practice with a partner, and it could be a friend, your parents, etc.

This might take days to practice, find the time and you will perfect it. And feel confident and ready for the interview you have been planning and preparing for.

The day of the interview, arrive 15 minutes early. When you come to the lobby, be social with the front desk when you sign in

TIP: if you are able, wait in the lobby standing up; facing away from where the Interviewer will great you from.

The reason for this, found it to be awkward when the interviewer is coming towards me from a distance. Also found it uncomfortable to be sitting down, when I stood up, I had to re-adjust my jacket and put what I had on my lap down on the table or seat next to me. That extra movement might make me look incompetent.

During the interview, some companies are unscripted. Not all companies have their Recruiting practices the same. They are slightly different from company to company; you will notice the pattern at a high level. Next thing you will see you become agile and able to respond to any questions these companies have because you practiced both the non-situational and Behavioral and Situational interviews.

There are times that unplanned questions pop up that you did not anticipate. While interviewing with the Recruiter or hiring manager, they add a specific new job requirement that they MUST have, that was never on your resume.

In these situations, you can't help but get a bit upset because they are anchored in having these new job criteria as a requirement, and you have gone out of You're way to move your calendar and schedule around to accommodate the interview. Do not want to lose your cool, maintain your professional. If you do not have that new criteria, merely say, "That was not on my resume, however, I am always willing to learn if you give me an opportunity."

On the positive side, there are times that the Recruiter or Hiring managers, after the interview, might ask if you would consider a job you did not apply for. Sometimes after talking to you and getting to know you, they see you be a better fit for more than one open position. Always say yes, you are willing to explore other opportunities. They would not ask if you were not the right fit. You might have to interview again with another group, which is OK, you got your foot in the door and a new opportunity.

TIP: your body language during the interview is to be professional.

a. Keep your posture straight
b. Do not touch your face
c. Look relax
d. Have a pad and paper on hand ready to take notes so you can look attentive and so you can recap what they were saying.
e. Mirror the interviewer's body language, for example, if they lean back, you lean back.
f. Eye contact; look at the interviewer in the eyes.
g. Smile, look at them in the eyes, and show your teeth. The key is to be genuine.

You want to get them to like you, trust you and value you, and your behavior can contribute to them loving you. After the interview, the last question will be "do you have any questions for us." Always say yes, have your questions ready this way you do not say "um" it shows you were not prepared. You should have an idea of some open questions; the interviewer has not talked about. If they answered all your questions, have at least a couple for them.

Here are some examples of questions to ask:

1. Is the position newly created position or is it replacing an existing person?
2. Is there travel, if so how often?
3. Where do you see your department in the next three years?
4. What are your expectations of this role?
5. In this position, can this role work remote?

TIP: Have your questions written down in your note pad so you can refer to them. It will show that you are interested and proactive.

Three MUST questions:

1. How soon are you looking to fill in the position?
2. What are the next steps?
3. When should I expect to hear from you?
4. When you all are done, and you get walked out, be sure to thank them, shake their hands. And say this:
5. I want this job, and I believe I am the perfect fit for this job; I am confident I can meet and achieve the objectives for this role.

Wait to see what they say. You will catch them off guard, but it tells them you are super motivated for the job, and that is what employers want. As they walk you out to the lobby or pass security be engaged in small talk. Casual small conversation removes awkwardness and makes you more likable. It is about being polite and showing interest.

Here are some ideas of small talk when being escorted out after the interview:

1. Nice office, is it recently remodeled
2. It is a beautiful view from this floor
3. That is an exciting display, is it on all the floors?
4. Do you have casual Fridays in this office?
5. How long have you been working to here?
6. Hope your commute is not bad (best asked toward the end of the day when people are ready to go home)
7. Everyone is so nice here.

In short, getting ready for the interview is one step closer to getting the job you want. This is where first impressions matter. There are two things you want to impress people with, and you want them to trust and value you. The clothes you wear to the interview, your behavior and what you say can win them over. This is where the practice you put in, is of significant value, what and how you respond to the questions will show that your responses come naturally to you; it will be interpreted as you being very knowledgeable because you did not stutter with the subject. That is a value; you got something they do not have. Always be prepared for the unplanned questions.

The practicing will let you prepare for those questions you did not expect, like do you have another type of experience besides for the job you are interviewing for, or would you be interested in another open position. You ask questions during and after the interviews show you are interested in the post, always have questions for the interviewers. Walk away with confidence, getting ready for the meeting will prepare you for what you practiced. Now it is about waiting for the next steps in the recruiting process.

After the interview

You made it, the interview is over, and there are a few things to do next. One sends them a thank you letter, and follow up with the Recruiter.

Thank you letter

- This is an option and your call, if you want to send a follow-up email to the hiring manager or panel you interviewed with, do so with a Thank you letter.
- If you have their email address, which could be listed in the Interview Meeting Calendar, or if you have their business card, yes you can send them a thank you Letter.
- In today's environment, it is not expected, however, a nice to have. I say this because it depends on the culture of the company.
- For example, if you were interviewing for a prestige, traditional, and large organization where formality is part of

the culture, then sending a Thank you Letter would be a good idea.

If you are interviewing at a manufacturing company, a start-up, family-owned company, then they do not expect it or even have time to read it.

In either event, it is a good idea to send the Interviewers a Thank you letter using a business format; it will show that you are interested. The letter should be short and should cover:

Greetings: Dear John Smith,

- A body of the email to include three parts:

  One: thanking them for their time

  Two: what you learned from meeting with them

  Three: how you are the perfect fit for the position and tie both what they are looking for with your resume.

- I look forward to hearing from you soon
- Best regards,

TIP: Carbon Copy "cc" the recruiter in your thank you letter.

When you do not get the job, one possible reason could be the company had an idea who they wanted to hire.

You will know you did not get the job when:

- You do not hear back from the recruiter
- You get a rejection email or letter.
- Sometimes you will not get either of the above.

There are cases where you are a fit for the company. However, the company already knew who they were going to hire for the position, even before the job requisition was posted—not all but some.

For example, I have gone to interviewers where an internal (e.g., contractor, or employee) is working performing the function of the job posted. The Manager goes thru the recruiting process, to make it appear they are fair when their real intent is to hire the internal person (e.g., internal employee, contractor). I do not think that is fair for those candidates who were qualified and were asked to take time out of their day/s to come into the office to interview. The lack of integrity and respect of others. I call back the recruiter and ask why I was not selected, the recruiter stated, "they hired the internal contractor they are working with currently."

Lessons Learned: If you do not hear back from the company or if the company ended up hiring someone else, call the Recruiter.

- Ask why you were not selected. Do not sound confrontational, you merely want to know what you could have done better.
- When you call them to say,

"Hello Recruiter, this is John Smith, I understand you filled the position with another candidate, however, I would like the opportunity to learn what qualifications I was missing and want to learn to improve myself for the next opportunity."

Some recruiters will call you, do not be surprised if they tell you they can't help you or provide you feedback. It is better to ask that never ask.

What's after the interview, well send a thank you letter. A thank you note lets the interviewers know you are interested. Use a business format for your Thank you letter, and include the typical salutations and three parts: One: thanking them for their time; Two: what you learned from meeting with them; and Three: how you are the perfect fit for the position and tie both what they are looking for with your resume. If you do get the Rejection notification email or letter that you did not get the job, call the Recruiter. Ask the recruiter you want to do a lesson learned, and want to know what you could have done better.

Exercise

Write your interview questions and responses.

_____

_____

_____

_____

_____

_____

_____

_____

_____

_____

_____

Write your Email Thank you letter.

_____

_____

_____

_____

_____

_____

_____

_____

_____

Chapter 11

How do you Answer In-Person Interview Questions?

Prepare…you want to feel confident after an interview; you want to feel good because you prepared to the best of your ability. By being prepared it reduces your anxiety and had eliminated any doubts you might have had if you were underprepared. After the interview you do not want to ask yourself, "I could have said this…" or "I should not have said this…" To get rid of those feelings, you must be prepared and ready for this In-Person Interview. At the end of the phone interview, YOU want to be the leading job candidate in this pool of competition of getting the job you want.

First, know yourself, and know the company's Products, industry, tools, systems, everything you can think of that you must know how to do a GREAT job that will add Business value to that company you want to work for.

Know your:

- Skills
- Resume
- Performance appraisal/evaluations history.

- Reflect on those and write down your accomplishments.

TIP: write down your winning attributes and accomplishment. It will make it easier to remember when telling a situational scenario during the interview process.

- Personal Achievements file, for example, projects you worked on, awards and recognitions received, and school or professional course taken.
- Know your accomplishments, have the memorized and have an Elevator Speech for each achievement.
- Elevator Speech: is a one, or two-minute story you can tell about your education, experience and accomplishments.

For example, at my prior employer received a Recognition Award for saving 5 million dollars by developing and implementing an automated Audit Process.

Strengths are significant; everyone has massive talents and strengths. Knowing your strengths will differentiate you from your competition. Make it easier for you to talk about your strengths, and how your strengths have added business value to your past and current workplaces.

Values, needs, and expectations.

Know your Job Market

You should be at a point you've done enough research to know your market. What I mean by knowing your market is: If you are an accountant, you should be up to date on accounting guidelines (i.e., GAAP and FASB), education and industry trends.

TIP: Every week read articles, white papers, case studies, etc. Related to the field you are in, it will keep you up to date on the latest trends.

Know your market by what company's and company divisions are seeking in terms of candidates, the job requirements, the company or even departments goals, by reading about the market you will pick up any particular projects challenges (all this is could have been covered in articles or industry leaders such as TED talks, etc.) a company is facing. You can also know about the company, the company's values, culture, and expectations by reading the company's job site.

For example, if you are an electrical engineer, part of your market research should include what is going on globally by knowing what other energy, electrical companies, and energy problems they are trying to solve, or innovations they have created. This Industry Insight might come in handy during the interview.

Know how well you are a match to the position:

- Map your skills with the position you are interviewing for
- Map your experience to the industry
- Map your education
- Identify the companies' vision, values, and direction and see how well it matches your interest to grow and how you can add business value to achieve the companies' goals.
- Match the job posting to YOU

The above steps are critical steps in preparing for the job interview. It makes you well informed and fully aware of everything about the job.

TIP: you must prove you are a perfect match, during the interview you will repeat and restate how you are doing the same things that they are looking for the position. This can be done by using the Keywords, memorize the keywords this way it comes out naturally during the interview, You do not want to struggle by using "UMM" in attempt to remember what their critical words for the job are.

The first In-Person interview is typical with the Recruiter.

There are several ways this will occur:

1. The Recruiter can ask you the questions in a In Phone Interview, or
2. The Recruiter will ask you to come in without a In-Phone interview screening.

In either event, expect this:

The Recruiter will not know the specifics details of the job or even know about the department and team members. The Recruiters goal is to do a phone interview screening, and they will want to know the following and asking these questions:

*   Tell me why you are looking for a job
*   What do you know about our company
*   Tell me why you want to work here.
*   What made you interested in the position

TIP: Before the interview, have these four questions written down with one or two sentences with your responses, have these in front of you, ready so when they ask the questions, you are ready and reply with confidence. You will notice this will flow out of you naturally.

Examples:

*   Tell me why you are looking for a job

    Response: *I am happy at my current employer, however, saw your position and felt I was a perfect match.*

*   What do you know about our company

    Response: *I know that (name their company) revenues were $ (find out what their earning were) dollar and produced (name the product and services offered).*

I know Bank of xxx revenue for 2019 grew by 4% to 87 Billion in assets and offer products and services globally and locally.

- Tell me why you want to work here.

   Response: *Saw the position and it is in alignment with my experience and training. The focus on (*start using keywords in their job description) is the same objectives that I am focused on at my current and past employers.*

- What made you interested in the position

   Response: *I was excited to see the position; first it is what I am doing now, the difference I get to (start using the keywords in their job description) which is on track to what I do best.*

Where I state: *start using keywords in their job description, I mean that companies use different words to say the same thing by speaking their language, use their jargon, this way they intuitively and subconsciously they feel assured you will fit right in. Use their terminology because companies, like people, are mean the same thing, but using different words.

Getting Ready for the Interview Homework:

In this table are questions typically asked during an interview; and possible responses. The idea is to get you started by providing the an outline on how to start the Response, the rest you can fill in based on the resume and the job you applied for.

Interview Questions table:

Question	Response
What did you do in your last or current company	In my current company, I xyz...start filling in the blanks.
Tell me about yourself	I am xyz... start filling in the blanks.
Why should I hire you	I am the perfect fit for this job, I xyz... start filling in the blanks with what is relevant
What are your strengths	Xyz... start filling in the blanks with your positive attributes (e.g. clear communications that allows me to xyz)
What is your weakness	I am not patient for task that are not completed by others, I tend to follow up daily with those individuals until the task is completed, xyz... start filling in the blanks with what is relevant
Why are you a good fit for this position	I am a good fit, my xyz... start filling in the blanks with what is relevant to the job

After you write them, print them out or have them handy at all times, and start practicing.

- First, practice by memorizing what you wrote.
- Second, practice in front of a mirror without looking at your paper, iPhone, or queue cards, or whatever you feel comfortable with.
- Third, practice with a partner; ask a friend or relative to ask you the questions.

TIP: the responses do not have to be a paragraph long; could be as short as two sentences. Recruiters and hiring managers have a short retention span because they have a tone of work they are thinking about and want to get through this process to mark it done in their checklist.

Each time you practice, you will see the practice makes a difference. Compared to your first practice, practice with your partner, you will notice the words to your responses flow out naturally. That is what you want.

TIP: Before the Interview, you must do your Research on the company you are about to talk to or meet with go to:

- Glassdoor.com for company reviews, salary, company culture
- LinkedIn.com for specific person review
- Company website
- Products made
- Revenue generated per year
- Number of employees both domestic and globally
- Competitors
- Review job description

Insider Secret: Align your past milestone with job requirements

- Use your milestones as talking points to show a value
- Research line items that are new technology used in a role

TIP: Understand and convey the value you bring:

To the company, and, to the team, one suggestion is to tell them something they do not know, remember you have been doing the research making them more aware of what is the trend and what is going on in the industry. Memorize or have written down at least five critical facts about.

The interviewer and the team are busy doing their job, and they do not have time to do the kind of research you have been doing.

Demonstrate your VALUE by letting them knows what the trend is, and how you can help them bring Value.

In-Person Interview Ice Breakers

What are interviews icebreakers, when you first met a person, you do not jump into your personal life? The same thing applies when interviewing, when you first encounter with the Recruiter or hiring manager, you do not dive into the details of the job you are talking or the job you are doing now. You want to have a natural start, to get that rapport established. You want to create an environment where the interviewer feels comfortable and can have a sense of trust.

Icebreakers can start with simple open questions, as the person being interview ask "how is your day going" this is a chance for the Recruiter or manager know that you are an engaging person and want to know you are thoughtful and considerate.

One question that all Recruiters and Managers will ask you is "Tell me about yourself" It is their # 1 Ice Breaker. In every single interview that I have personally had, it has been asked 100% of the time. So be ready, and have your response memorized.

TIP: you will need to change your response by a little, that way during your reply you say the keywords from their job description you are interviewing for.

Believe it or not, by having your responses memorized, it reduces interview anxiety and helps build confidence. You want to give a good first impression, and your response matters in the interview. The reason is, sometimes the Recruiter or hiring manager has not read thru your resume, they prefer you to tell them about yourself, instead of them reading your resume. Your resume was filtered by the HR System, and put on the Recruiters or Hiring Managers HR System work queue (aka wordlists) as a percentage match to the criteria they needed for the job.

Have these key points ready to address in your first essential questions in the interview that will be asked:

- How many years of experience do you have in this industry?
- Summary of: How long were you with your current and prior companies with; and, an overview of the various jobs and critical projects or initiatives you worked on.
- Point out measures such as how money or time you have saved the company.

Education

You earned a degree or certificate in these areas or fields, which contributed to having an edge in the company because of your learning in that area or field you were educated on. Relevant skills and experience, try to align the job description with yours to voice out the similarities between your prior jobs and the job you are interviewing for. Lastly, end the statement with: I believe I am a fit for the position for XYZ.

You Pass the Interview:

After the conversations with the Recruiter, and with the series of questions are asked, a couple of things will happen.

Moving to the next step, Interview with the Hiring Manager.

The recruiter will ask you for your availability for another last interview with the Hiring Manager. Once you provide your date and times, the recruiter will follow up with an email to confirm the next in person or phone interview with the hiring manager.

Respond to confirm interview(s):

When you receive the email confirmation respond via email. Respond right away; recruiters are overwhelmed with work if you wait they might forget the conversation you just had.

Here are some response examples.

Email	Response
Email confirmation for next interview	Hello (recruiter name), It was great talking to you today. I am very excited about the position. Look forward meeting (or talking) to the hiring manager (name) on Date/Time (type in actual date/time). Best regards, Your name
Email confirmation for next interview – schedule conflict	Hello (recruiter name), It was great talking to you today. Here is my availability: Monday, 11/1/20xx 10:00AM to 1:00PM PST Friday, 11/3, 8:00AM to 10:00AM PST Tuesday, 11/14, 4:00PM to 5:00PM Look forward hearing from you. Best regards, Your name

Tip: This process can be applied at any stage of the Interview Process and is recommended as a good practice to apply Response to confirm interviews at any stage of the interview process.

Recruiters are Busy:

There are times that the Recruiter might not see your email response because they are so busy if you want you can, call the recruiter and leave a voice mail message telling them you have responded to their email confirming the interview for this Date and time with this Hiring Manager.

The recruiter will provide respond with more details, and they will recap what the job is for, who you will be meeting with, offer you the address and directions. If they do not, you ask them for those details or not given to you up front.

For example, this has happened to me. An agenda was given to me in advance, notice that the plan had me double booked, so I replied to the recruiter and told them I was double booked between two managers---they corrected it. It is OK to challenge the recruiter or whoever is sending you information, if the information they provided does not seem right, let them know.

Take care of YOU:

Interviews are not always about the company, it is about you, and your time is valuable. You are changing your daily routine to meet with this company. You are making special arrangements, to make sure you can do the interview. You are calling in sick, asking for a vacation day, making child care arrangement, or even driving a longer distance than you usually do to make it to the interview. Your time matter and you want to make the best of it, to get the job you want.

In summary, after the phone screen, the next steps are the coordination between you and the recruiter. The exchange in email or phone conversations secures you a spot for the interview. In the exchange of information, email is preferred, it provides the instructions of when you are to have your meeting, which you are to meet with and where you are to be. If you see a typo or if the information the recruiter provided does not appear correctly—let them know. You want to be sure you are there on time, meeting with the right people and the given location. You are in charge; your time is valuable, you want to get it right to get that job you want.

We also talked about getting ready for the interview. Preparing for the interview will increase your success rate of moving forward to the next phase of the interview process, and make you a leading candidate and being ready means being prepared by knowing what is important and relevant to the job you are interviewing for. Know yourself, your market, and your career accomplishments. Know the position you are talking for and what you put on your resume for the resume you submitted. Lastly, be ready to respond to the questions that are familiar with the issues the Recruiter or Hiring manager will be asking. Anticipate the problems, and memorize your responses, this will help you answer them with ease, and it will increase your confidence level and remove the anxiety of interviewing.

Exercise

Write down why you are looking for a job?

Write down three Keywords you should mention in your In-Person Interview.

Why should your interview responses be as short as two sentences?

Chapter 12
You Got The Job!

S o you get a call from the Recruiter: if you recognize the phone number and you happen to be in a right place, take the call. If you happen to be at work or in a meeting, have the call go directly to voice mail and return the call when you are in a private and quiet place where you can talk. When a Recruiter calls you back after the interview with the Hiring manager that means two things:

One: they are calling you to make the job offer.

Two: they need to know your salary requirements before the job offer.

If you did not cover the salary requirements up front with the recruiter, you should have a good idea of what the market is paying for the job you applied for because you did all your upfront research and analysis. If the Recruiter is calling back to see what your salary requirement are referred back to this Question and answer table.

Question and Answer table

Question	Answer	Insider Secret
What is your salary requirement	"What is your salary Range?" Once they reply say this: a) Yes that is within my range. b) No, based on the duties, the range is too low, can we go up to $$$$$. Can we meet in the middle? Might be able to work with it if I could work remote 2 days out of the week.	Do not say the first number; have them give the salary range. You do not want to go to high or low. Only you know what you need, if you do not have anything, you might say yes, totally up to you. Or even ask to go a little higher. If you have a job, and the move is a promotion, weigh your options of the pros and cons. To see if it worth getting a new job. If the salary is to low, see if they can flexible, by giving you extra paid vacations, working remote, etc.

The next steps will be to accept the job offer by email from the Recruiter. The Recruiter will provide you with instructions after that, each set of guidelines have deadlines.

Things to expect:

- Complete the Job application information, needed to conduct the employment and the educational background check
- Complete the Drug test instructions; you will need to take some time to go to a facility. Typically you have three days to complete the drug test.

TIP: do not quite your job until you receive an official letter from the Recruiter that you have passed the background and drug test, and they confirm your start date and work location. Once you negotiate your salary, you accept the position and agree on a start date. The start date depends on your situation.

Situation one: If you have a job and you want to give two-week courtesy notice, wait to give your resignation until you get the FINAL confirmation from the Recruiter. This FINAL confirmation will state that your background and drug test have passed. The FINAL confirmation will include: where to report, your manager's name; and the time you should appear at work. The background check and drug test takes up to two weeks, plan to start four weeks after your job offer, contingent upon the FINAL confirmation from your new company. After your FINAL confirmation, then you can give your two-week courtesy notice. By then your new job is secured, and you are ready to start.

Situation two: you are not employed, and can start in two weeks.

Situation three: you are on vacation during the job employment, work it out with the Recruiter, and background check. Maybe you can start in six to seven weeks. This is entirely up to you. If you are relocating to a new state, you will need more time to pack up and get situated in your new home for your new job.

Get Ready for your new Position:

Now that you go the Job you wanted, there is more; you do not stop learning. You want to go in well prepared, start reading up on the company, what are their strengths, there challenges, what is the trend. If you know what tools and the area you will be working in. Lean in and learn to see what is going on in the industry, what are competitors are doing.

They are expecting you to add value your first day, and you want to be ready to contribute with the new knowledge base you have learned.

Congratulations you got the job offer! You get the call from the Recruiter; you negotiated your salary and start date to fit your situation. If you have a job, you do not quite it yet. You have to wait until you get the FINAL confirmation you passed all of their hiring verifications from your new employer. Getting the job is the most substantial part, next start getting ready for the new position by reading up on the company getting to know your new role with the new company.

Exercise

What is your salary requirement?

What are the two things to expect when you are onboarding into a new job?

What steps do you need to take after you accept the new job?

Chapter 13

How do you increase a Job Salary?

Before you start your job: When you start your new job search, part of your research is the salary range. As covered in Chapter five, part of your research and analysis is to know the salary range for the job you want, and this will give you a good sense of what to expect. It is in Chapter five that will help you determine your short list of jobs that meet your requirements, including the salary.

During the job application process In Chapter six, we covered the tips of the resume, another tip while applying; always take time to see what the market is paying. It changes slightly depending on the demand.

For example, use Indeed, Glassdoor.com to see what those types of jobs are paying.

Before the Job interview: Before you go to the meeting if the recruiter did not disclose the salary or ask you your salary requirements. Go back to Chapter 1 salary research, to get a good idea what the job you are interviewing is paying. Sometimes after the interview, they will ask what your salary requirements are.

TIP: do not say the first number, answer the question with a question: What is our salary range?

The Recruiter will tell you the range; if they do not know it, they will get it.

TIP: The Recruiter has the range when a new job is posted at a company; they need to have a salary range to make sure the position is in the department's budget. A budget is a dollar amount a department is given to spend.

Worse case, they will try to get a number from you. First, it is hard not to go low, try to stall by saying "I do not want to make less than I am today" This line sometimes works, and the Recruiter ends up giving you the first number.

If you are forced to give them a number, go HIGH. Give them a high range. If the recruiter says that is too high, then say: "I am flexible, can we meet in the middle?" Based on the Recruiter response, you can decide if it is something you want

Scenario 1 example:

- Your current situation is: Let's say you are currently making $60,000 year, but you commute two hours each way, and there is no growth in your current company.
- This job offer is for 60,000, and 10 minutes from home. It might be a consideration for you.
- There are pros/cons to what you are willing or able to accept as a salary. Weigh your options and write them down on paper. This will help you make a better decision.

In summary, always stay on top of what the market is paying for the job you want. You want a fair salary for the role and responsibility of the Job you are expected to perform. Part of your job research is to know what the market is paying, plus the compensation package (i.e., health insurance benefits, etc.). During the job search, when you get a call from a recruiter, always ask what the salary range is, and the expectations of the role. This is necessary to see if the salary is too low for the amount of work and responsibility expected. When it comes to the Salary Range, do not give the first number; let the Recruiter provide the name. Depending on the salary range you can weight your options, there are too many variables to consider when it comes to salary.

Exercise

What is the best way to negotiate a higher salary?

_____
_____
_____
_____
_____
_____
_____
_____

What other options can you negotiate other than a higher salary?

_____
_____
_____
_____
_____
_____
_____
_____

Fill in the following. Do not say the _____ number, answer the question with a question: What is our _____ range?

Chapter 14

You Got More Money!

When the question is asked, "what is your desired compensation, or what is your rate," comes up. **Number one rule**; you never give the first number. Let the person on the other line end give you their rate. This is why, when the job requisition was posted, one of the job posting requirements is to have a salary range. This is necessary for a couple of reasons:

- The salary must be approved by the department's manager, and It must be accepted and on the budget.

You ask them, "What is your salary range," and wait to see what they say, after that, you can decide if it meets what you wanted to earn.

- If it is within your range, respond, "It is within my range."
- If it is a job you are interested in because you want to get your foot in the door, they say, "it is too low. However, I am interested in the role."

Exercise

What is the number one rule when negotiating a higher salary?

_____

_____

_____

_____

_____

_____

_____

_____

What can you ask to discover the company's salary range?

_____

_____

_____

_____

_____

_____

_____

_____

If you want to get your foot in the_____, then say, "it is too _____, however, I am _____in the _____ "

Chapter 15

On to the next Job Opportunity

J ob Acceptance: Once the verbal offer is extended and you accept, wait for the email confirmation. You will not be sure you got the job until your application, screening, and drug test passes. You will have to wait for one final job confirmation from the hiring team that your background and drug test results passed. In the same communication, they will have your actual start date.

After you get the **FINAL** confirmation with our start date, then you can give your current employer a courtesy 2-week advance notice. **BE PREPARED**: Don't' be surprised if your current employer lets you go the same day you give notice. Be prepared. All companies have an at-will policy, and no notice is required. As soon as you accept and start your new job, prepare your exit strategy just in case your current employer escorts you out.

The job you are about to start with a new company is new. There are many unknowns about the people, culture and their ways of working. The first on your to-do list is to update your resume by adding your new job.

The reason for this, in the event the job is not what you expected. Have your resume ready to apply to a new job. Think of it as your back up plan. In your latest job, it will take 90 days for you to know if that company is where you want to work. It takes 90 days for you to understand the culture, the personalities, the way of working at the company. During the interview process, the company sells you on the company, after 90 days you will know if those expectations they conveyed where a half-truth and not completely honest.

For example, during the interview process I asked do you have this framework and policy in place, they said yes, we have it. By the time I joined I had discovered they had some of the framework, they were not practicing it. I got stuck being a teacher and hallway monitor to make sure people followed the guidelines. On top of the role I was hired to do, I ended up having to educate people on industry best practice that did not report to me.

- Sometimes they do not want to hear what is the right way to do things, so you end up being the bad guy and work with what they have and doing things there way.
- This was not a good sign if you are not learning anything new in the job; and if it is not going to help your next high paying job, you start rethink your longevity at the company.
- That is why it is essential to have an exit strategy. Do not do anything rash, and it is necessary to re-assess and take inventory to help you get ready for your next job, at the same time you want to keep that cash flow from your current situation until you plan out your exit strategy.

Exit Strategies:

1. If you are in a few weeks into your new job, and you are getting callbacks from Recruiters for the first and second round of interviews, Go to them if that is what you want.

2. If you are within the early 90 days into your new job, continue to apply and be selective as to whom you interview with. Only interview companies you deem worthy of value.

3. If you are a couple of weeks into your job and you get a new job offer from a previous company, you interviewed for, and it is for a similar situation and pay---**ACCEPT** the position. **DO NOT** Quite your job until you have the **FINAL** confirmation with your start date.

4. If the job is tolerable, and there is some value, stay at the current company for at least one year to give you that tenure. Then start applying for the new job you want to level up in your career.

Glossary

Most words have multiple meanings, so for a full understanding of each word included here, seek out a good dictionary. I have found that my ability to fully understand any subject is limited only by my knowledge of the words contained in that subject is limited only by my understanding of the words contained in that subject. So the first thing to do, the secret to applying the How To Get Hired Formula, is always to understand the words and phrases of the subject you are learning. This has been a critical point of my success. When I have failed to do this, I have failed in reaching my goals.

401(k). Retirements account to which both employee and employers contribute, on which taxes are deferred until withdrawal, and for which the employee usually selects the types of investments.

abundance. An ample quantity; wealth.

accomplish. (1) To bring about (a result) by effort; (2) to bring to completion; (3) to succeed.

act. The doing of a thing; deed.

action. (1) A thing done; deed; (2) the accomplishment of a thing usually over a period.

adapt. To make fit (as for a specific or new use or situation), often by modification.

additional. The result of adding; increase.

advertising. The action of calling something to the attention of the public, especially by paid announcements.

agreed. To concur in (as an opinion); admit, concede.

agreement. (1) A contract duly executed and legally binding; (2) spoken or unspoken mutual reality on a given situation.

annual. Covering the period of a year.

asset. An item of value owned; (plural) the items on a balance sheet showing the book value of property owned.

attention. (1) Observation, notice, especially a consideration with a view to action; (2) an act of civility or courtesy, especially in courtship; (3) consideration of the needs and wants of others

basic. Constituting or serving as the basis or starting point.

basics. Something that is fundamental (e.g., get back to *basics*).

blind. Made or done without sight of certain objects.

briefing. An act or instance of giving precise instructions or essential information.

broke. To ruin financially; out of money.

budget. A list of all planned expenses and revenues; a plan for saving and spending.

business downturn. A downward turn, especially toward a decline in business and economic activity.

campaign. A connected series of operations designed to bring about a particular result.

capital. (1) A stock of accumulated goods, especially at a specified time and in contrast to income received during a specified time and in contrast to income received during a specified period; also the value of these accumulated goods; (2) accumulated goods devoted to the production of other goods; (3) accumulated possessions calculated to bring in income.

circumstance. The sum of essential and environmental factors (as of an event or situation).

community. A body of persons of common and especially professional interests scattered throughout a larger society.

competition. Those who strive against others to win.

competitive. The state of striving consciously or unconsciously for an objective.

contact. A person serving as a go-between, messenger, connection, or source of special information.

courage. An act that demonstrates mental or moral strength to venture, persevere, and withstand danger, fear, or difficulty.

creative. Having the quality of something created rather than imitated.

critical. Of, relating to, or being a turning point or especially important juncture.

CRM (Customer Relations Manager).

Software applications that allow companies to manage every aspect of their relationship with a customer.

culture. (1) The set of shared attitudes, values, goals, and practices that characterizes an institution or organization (a corporate *culture* focused on the bottom line); (2) the set of values, conventions, or social practices associated with a particular field, activity, or societal characteristic.

cycle (hire cycle). An interval of time during which a recurring succession of events or phenomena are completed.

database. Usually a large collection of data organized especially for rapid search and retrieval.

database management. The act of conducting or supervising usually a large collection of data.

discipline. To train or develop by instruction and exercise, especially in terms of self-control.

dominate. To take over, overpower, or bring into submission of another or others.

earn. (1) To become duly worthy of or entitled or suited to; (2) to make worthy of or obtain (e.g., *earn* your business).

economy. The structure or conditions relating to or based on the production, distribution, and consumption of goods and services.

endurance. The ability to withstand hardship or adversity, especially the ability to sustain a prolonged stressful effort or activity.

elevator speech: short description about yourself that explains your education, experience and accomplishments.

environment. The circumstances, objects, or conditions that surround a person.

experience. (1) Direct observation of or participation in events as a basis of knowledge; (2) the fact or state of having been affected by or gained knowledge through direct observation or participation.

FASB: Financial Accounting Standards Board "FASB" is a private, non-profit organization standard-setting body whose primary purpose is to establish and improve Generally Accepted Accounting Principles within the United States in the public's interest.

financial plan. A plan of how to stay solvent about income and expenses.

financial quarter. The first three months of a financial year.

GAAP: Generally Accepted Accounting Principles "GAAP" is the accounting standard adopted by the U.S. Securities and Exchange Commission.

generate. To create or be the cause of (a situation, action, or state of mind).

goals. To create or be the cause of (a situation, action, or state of mind).

guarantee. An assurance for the fulfillment of condition such as an agreement by which one person undertakes to secure another in the possession or enjoyment of something.

IBM (International Business Machines Corporation). Is an American multinational information technology company. IBM produces and sells computer hardware, middleware, and software, and provides hosting and consulting services in areas ranging from mainframe computers to nanotechnology.

invest. To involve or engage, especially emotionally (e.g., *invest* time and energy).

know. (1) To perceive directly; have direct cognition of; (2) to have understanding of; to recognize the nature of; to discern; to recognize as being the same as something previously known; (3) to be acquainted or familiar with; (4) to have experience of; to be aware of the truth or factuality of; to be convinced or certain of; to have a practical understanding of.

knowledge. The fact or condition of knowing something with familiarity gained through experience or association; acquaintance with or understanding of a science, art, or technique; the fact or condition of being aware of something; the range of one's information or understanding.

momentum. Strength or force gained by motion or through the development of events.

money. Something generally accepted as a medium of exchange, a measure of value, or a means of payment, such as officially coined or stamped currency.

must. (1) To be commanded or requested to (e.g., you *must* stop); (2) be urged to; ought by all means to.

objection. (1) A reason or argument presented in opposition; (2) a feeling or expression of disapproval.

participate. (1) To take part; (2) to have a part or share in something.

perfect. To make perfect; improve or refine.

positive. (1) Having a good effect; favorable (e.g., a *positive* role model); (2) marked by optimism (e.g., the *positive* point of view).

problems. (1) A source of perplexity, distress, or vexation; (2) difficulty in understanding or accepting; (3) opposition to a solution.

profit. The excess of returns over expenditure in a transaction or series of transactions; especially the excess of the selling price of good over their cost.

profitable. Affording profits; yielding advantages returns or results.

purpose. (1) Something set up as an object or end to be attained; an intention; (2) resolution; determination.

qualify. To declare competent or adequate. In sales, it means determining a person's financial ability.

quarter. One of four three-month divisions in a year.

quit. (1) To cease normal, expected, or necessary action; (2) to give up employment; (3) to admit defeat; to give up.

reasonable. (1) Being in accordance with reason (a *reasonable* theory); (2) not extreme or excessive.

referral. The act, action, or an instance of referring.

relationship. (1) The relation connecting or binding participants in a relationship; (2) a specific instance or type of kinship.

response. Something constituting a reply or a reaction.

resume. A document that contains a summary or listing of a person's relevant job experience and education. The resume or CV (curriculum vitae) is typically the first item that a potential employer encounters regarding a job seeker and is typically used to screen applicants. An application screening is often followed by an interview. (Don't ever rely on a resume without taking the time to meet the person who wants to hire you.)

revenue. The total income produced by given source.

schedule. Timetable for a program or project showing how activities and milestone events are sequenced and phased over the allotted period.

selective. (1) The act of being judicious or restrictive in choice; discriminating; (2) highly specific in activity.

service. Contribution to the welfare of others. The act of serving is a helpful act or is useful labor that does not produce a tangible commodity but benefits all parties involved in some way.

skill. (1) The ability to use one's knowledge effectively and readily in execution or performance, dexterity, or coordination, especially in the execution of learned physical tasks; (2) a learned power of doing something competently; (3) a developed aptitude or ability.

social networking. Online communities of people who share interests and/or activities or who are interested in exploring the interest and activities of others. Most social network services are Web-based and provide a variety of ways for users to interact, such as by e-mail and instant messaging.

solution. (1) An action or process of solving a problem; (2) an answer to a problem.

spend. (1) To pay money, usually in exchange for goods or services; (2) to use a resource, such as time.

standards. Something set up and established by authority as a rule for the measure of quantity, weight, extent, value, or quality.

success. Attaining a target or targets that a person has set for him- or herself. According to this author, there are three factors to success: it is important, it is your obligation, and there can never be a shortage of it.

thrive. (1) To grow vigorously; flourish; (2) to gain in wealth or possessions; prosper; (3) to progress toward or realize a goal despite of or because of circumstances.

training. (1) The act, process, or method of one who trains; (2) the skill, knowledge, or experience acquired by one who trains.

unemployment rate. Percentage of the total workforce who are unemployed and are looking for a paid job. Unemployment rate is one of the most closely watched statistics because a rising rate is seen as a sign of a weakening economy that may call for a cut in interest rates. Likewise, a falling unemployment rate indicates a growing economy, which is usually accompanied by a higher inflation rate and may call for an increase in interest rates.

value. Relative worth, utility, or importance.

value-add. Creation of competitive advantage by bundling, combining, or packaging features and benefits that result in greater customer acceptance.

wealth. (1) Tangible or intangible thing that makes a person, family, or group better off; (2) abundance of valuable material possessions or resources.

About the Author's

Austin Kelly

An internationally recognized Marketing Manager 5 + years experience working in the consumer goods industry creating campaigns for products featured on Target.com, Home Depot and Walmart.com. Austin Kelly received his Bachelors Degree in 2012 from the Pennsylvania State University College of Communications in University Park, PA, and began  his career with Electronic Arts project Star Wars Battle Front Online Video Game. His leadership and proven track record in North America working for Fortune 100 companies in the management and marketing of digital media campaigns began with the wisdom and guidance of his mother Gabriela Kelly who shares her expertise nationwide for everyone from senior executives to recent college graduates achieve a higher degree of success in the workforce.

Visit www.AustinKellyBooks.com

Gabriela Kelly

With 20 + years working experience as a strategic leader with a proven track record in North America working for Fortune 100 companies in the installation and maintenance of information technology of Human Resource Solutions. Gabriela Kelly shares her expertise with her new books "How to Get Hired," blogging and YouTube Live interviews, Gabriela provides one-on-one coaching nationwide for everyone  from senior executives to recent graduates. Contact Gabriela via her website, www.GabrielaKelly.com.